DO HOWARD GARDNER'S
MULTIPLE INTELLIGENCES
ADD UP?

D1458342

Institute of Education

UNIVERSITY OF LONDON

Do Howard Gardner's multiple intelligences add up?

JOHN WHITE

PROFESSOR OF PHILOSOPHY

First published in 1998 by the
Institute of Education University of London,
20 Bedford Way, London WC1H 0AL
Tel: 020 7612 6000. Fax: 020 7612 6126
www.ioe.ac.uk

Reprinted 2000

Pursuing Excellence in Education

British Library Cataloguing in Publication Data:
a catalogue record for this publication is available
from the British Library

ISBN 0-85473-552-6

Produced in Great Britain by
Reprographic Services
Institute of Education University of London

Printed by Formara Limited
16 The Candlemakers, Temple Farm Industrial
Estate, Southend on Sea, Essex SS2 5RX

I1/0003-PEP No.3-1000

CONTENTS

FOREWORD

The 'multiple intelligences' defined by
the Harvard psychologist, Howard
Gardner, are the subject of scrutiny in
the third of the new series of
Perspectives on Education Policy
launched by the Institute of Education,
University of London. Professor John
White's philosophical critique is also
the second paper from the Institute's
recently formed Broader Perspectives
Unit, based within our History and
Philosophy Academic Group.

This third Perspectives paper follows
reflections on the curriculum of schools
and a post-Dearing analysis of higher
education. Professor White's critical
approach to the argument for multiple
intelligences opens up the debate in an
area of vital importance to school
effectiveness and improvement thereby
fulfilling the hope of our new series: to
inform and widen public debate on
subjects of concern in the field of
education.

PROFESSOR PETER MORTIMORE
Director, Institute of Education

April 1998

Do Howard Gardner's multiple intelligences add up?

JOHN WHITE
Professor of Philosophy of Education
Institute of Education University of London

Introduction

How many of your intelligences have you used today?

An odd question? Not to the students in an Australian school who pass this message on a board each day on their way out of the building. For their schooling is based, like that of a rapidly growing number of pupils in the USA, Britain and elsewhere, on the theory of Multiple Intelligences (MI) produced by the Harvard psychologist Howard Gardner.

Howard Gardner published his book *Frames of Mind* in 1983. In it he argued for the existence of a small number of relatively discrete 'intelligences' in human beings, combinable in different ways to form the intellectual repertoire of different individuals. Two of these, logico-mathematical intelligence and linguistic intelligence, are what IQ tests have focused on. But intelligence is more multiplex than this: other intelligences include the musical, the spatial, the bodily-kinaesthetic, the intrapersonal and the interpersonal. His recent research has added to the original seven both the classificatory intelligence of the naturalist and – he has some doubts on this one – spiritual intelligence. He says, half seriously, that while Socrates viewed human beings as rational animals, he himself sees them as animals possessing eight-and-a-half intelligences (Craft, 1997:6).

The impact of MI theory on school reform

A discussion in 1998 of a 15-year-old theory may appear belated. I engage in it only because Gardner's views about multiple intelligences have grown increasingly influential over the years. He is now one of the best known experts on intelligence not only in America but across the world, and a leading contributor to the debates on Herrnstein's and Murray's *The Bell Curve* (1994). In addition, thousands of so-called 'MI schools' have sprung up in recent years in America, Canada, Australia and elsewhere, all based on his theory. Some of Gardner's disciples, as in the Australian example with which we began, believe that the curriculum should be based on the development of all the 'intelligences'. Gardner himself (1993:71) sees more educational mileage in recognizing that pupils 'have quite different minds from each other', and that 'education should be so sculpted that it remains responsive to these differences'.

His ideas are also currently influential in Britain. His notion of multiple intelligences is widely referred to by those involved in school reform, both at school and local authority level, and in educational research. In particular, MI theory has recently become a liberating force in school improvement projects across the country, from Sandwell and Birmingham in the West

Midlands to Govan in Scotland. It is not difficult to see why such a notion should appeal to teachers and policy-makers working in deprived areas and faced with underachievement. Many children in these areas are held back by a low self-concept. They see themselves as dim or thick. But this is within the framework of the traditional version of intelligence – they are poor at the kind of abstract logical thinking that IQ tests target. Broaden the picture and their perceptions are transformed. 'Children are born smart', as a project leader from Birmingham puts it. Their abilities may lie in physical activities, in music, in the visual arts, in interactions with other people. Extended learning schemes in West Midland, Glasgow and other schools tap into these and other areas. Once children become aware of how intelligent they are in this field or that, their self-esteem is said to increase amazingly. A project worker from Sandwell put it to Howard Gardner like this: 'The strength we get from your work is that you do use the word "intelligence", because the kids have been told so often – not explicitly, but they have picked up the message that they are not intelligent, that they don't have this chunk of intelligence' (Craft, 1997:19).

None of the projects mentioned is slavishly attached to Gardner's theory. They all use it more as a catalyst for unlocking pupils' – and parents' – minds. This is just as well, because the theory itself is decidedly flaky.

The idea of intelligence: introductory remarks

I suspect that many of Gardner's supporters on the ground have had, as busy people, little opportunity to go through his theory with a toothcomb. The idea that intelligence is not restricted to abilities tested by IQ tests but is found in all sorts of areas has wide appeal in the education world. It is a vital support in the work that teachers do in trying to overcome pupils' perceptions that they are unintelligent. But so far this has nothing specifically to do with Gardner's theory of MI. We should distinguish between the general claim that intelligence takes many different forms – not being restricted to the kind tested by IQ tests – and the particular version of this claim embodied in MI theory. The former is not new – and neither

3

was it new in 1983. In *The Concept of Mind* (1949) Ryle had reminded us that 'the boxer, the surgeon, the poet and the salesman' possess their own kinds of intelligent operation, applying 'their special criteria to the performance of their special tasks' (p.48). And more than 2,000 years ago Aristotle had distinguished the merely clever person, who is good at adapting means to ends whether the ends are desirable or not, from the practically wise person, who makes sure the ends are good to start with. There can, after all, be intelligent torturers and intelligent train robbers.

Intelligent action has to do with the flexible adaptation of means in the pursuit of one's goals and there are as many types of human intelligence as there are types of human goal. Intelligence is displayed in countless different ways. A bowler wants to get the batsman out, so he varies his delivery. A motorist on the M1 wants to get home safely and adjusts her speed, lane and signals appropriately to road conditions. Intelligence has nothing particularly to do with logical or mathematical thinking – or even with academic subjects more broadly conceived. We all draw on it every day in the practical tasks and projects that make up most of our lives. We want to sort out a family holiday and think through different possibilities. We want to split up with our partner and wonder how most painlessly we can do it. As citizens, we want a housebuilding policy but are worried about the environment – so what is the best way through?

Once unbewitched by IQ, we should find all this familiar enough. Gardner has always admitted the great number of different ways in which intelligence is manifested, yet has sought to regiment this variousness, to corral it within a small number of categories, within what he has called his 'charmed circle of intelligences' (Gardner 1983:60). The seven (in later versions, eight or more) intelligences are the relatively autonomous basic building blocks for all the rest, several of them participating in the boxer's skill, another combination of them in the surgeon's, and so on.

Later we will come back in more detail to the ordinary concept of intelligence and its connection with IQ. Meanwhile, we will look at the basic assumptions on which MI theory rests.

Gardner's Multiple Intelligence theory: a critique

CRITERIA OF AN INTELLIGENCE

What criteria guide Gardner in distinguishing his areas of intelligence? They embrace the following (1983:62-9):

- the potential isolation of the area by brain damage
- the existence in it of idiots savants and other exceptional individuals
- an identifiable core operation/set of operations
- a distinctive developmental history, along with a definable set of expert 'end-state' performances
- evolutionary history and plausibility
- support from experimental psychological tasks
- support from psychometric findings
- susceptibility to encoding in a symbol system.

As well as satisfying a range of these criteria, candidates for the title 'an intelligence' must – as a prerequisite – include problem-solving skills which are useful and important within a cultural context. The ability to recognize faces, for instance, passes many of the specific tests above, but 'does not seem to be highly valued by cultures' (p.61). The same is true of abilities tied to our gustatory or olfactory senses.

Gardner claims that the application of these criteria and this prerequisite distinguish the seven intelligences in his original account.

This presents the bones of Gardner's theory. I realize that several key terms, both those describing the criteria and those labelling the intelligences, have thus far been left unexplained, but I will fill out many of them as we proceed.

The question now is : is MI theory well-founded?

5

IMPORTANCE WITHIN A CULTURE

To start with the prerequisite that an intelligence must be important within a culture. Why is linguistic intelligence in, but the ability to recognize faces out? This seems counterintuitive. For if most of us – certainly in any modern culture and perhaps in any – lacked the ability to recognize the faces of our relatives, friends, colleagues, pupils or political leaders, it is hard to see how communal life as we know it would be possible. When Gardner says that this ability 'does not seem to be highly valued by cultures', I think he must mean that it is not a central constituent of *a highly valued social practice*. Linguistic intelligence is different. This has as its 'core operations' (see the list of criteria) a sensitivity to the meaning of words, to order among words, to the sounds and rhythms of words, and to the functions of language (p.77). These core operations are seen at work 'with special clarity' in the poet. Poetry is a highly valued social practice in many cultures and depends on the linguistic sensitivities just mentioned. There is no parallel social practice which depends on our capacity to recognize faces.

'A DISTINCTIVE DEVELOPMENTAL HISTORY'

If this is right, then there are highly valued social practices embedded in each intelligence. *How* are they embedded? At this point we must bring in another of Gardner's criteria, the possession of 'a distinctive developmental history, along with a definable set of expert "end-state" performances'. Linguistic intelligence, for instance, develops from less mature to more mature stages. Piaget is, as Gardner acknowledges, one of the central influences on his theory, and the idea of individuals' intellectual abilities unfolding through developmental stages is central to Gardner's own theory, in the domain of linguistic intelligence no less than in his other areas. There are two poles of such development: innately given abilities or sensitivities at one end, their full flowering at the other. In the linguistic case, following Chomsky (Gardner 1983:80), we begin with sensitivity to the meanings of words and the other sensitivities mentioned above. These develop into more sophisticated linguistic abilities and find their highest expression in poetry.

Other intelligences illustrate the same point. 'Musical intelligence involves the capacities for imitation of vocal targets, for sensitivity to relative as well as absolute pitch, and for appreciating various kinds of musical transformation' (Gardner, 1990:934). Again, we have genetically wired-in capacities at one pole and the highest flights of musical genius at the other. Spatial intelligence develops from such core abilities as perceiving the visual world accurately, performing transformations on one's visual experience, and recreating aspects of the latter (Gardner, 1983:173). The highly valued social practices at the mature pole are painting, sculpture and the sciences. Similar claims are made about the remaining intelligences – logico-mathematical, bodily-kinaesthetic, intrapersonal and interpersonal.

Gardner's theory of intelligence is developmentalist. Developmentalism, as I am using the term here, is the theory that the biological unfolding between two poles from seed through to mature specimen that we find in the physical world – e.g. of plants, or human bodies – is also found in the mental world. Piaget's theory, which has influenced Gardner, is one type of developmentalism – one which lays more stress on the contribution of the environment, including the social environment, than some other views (Hamlyn, 1978:ch.4). In his criteria, Gardner acknowledges the two poles in the mental case. At one end, there are allegedly genetically given capacities common to human beings like visual perception, sensitivity to the meanings and sounds of words, the ability to move our bodies in different ways etc. This is why research into the localization of mental functions in different parts of the brain plays such an important part in Gardner's thinking and why potential isolation of a mental area through brain damage provides one of his criteria: if there are specific areas for this function or that, then these functions belong to our innate biological equipment. At the other end of the developmental process is the mature state, the 'definable set of expert "end-state" performances' mentioned among the criteria. We have already seen such examples of expertise in the highest flights of poetry, music, painting, sculpture and science. Intrapersonal intelligence, whose core capacity or mental seed is 'access to one's own feeling life', finds its full development in the work of a novelist like Proust or the patient or therapist 'who comes to attain a deep knowledge of his feeling life' (1983:239). Interpersonal intelligence, arising out of the primitive 'ability to notice and make distinctions among other individuals' generates its 'highly developed forms...in political and religious leaders (a Mahatma Gandhi or a Lyndon Johnson), in skilled parents and teachers' etc. (ibid).

PROBLEMS IN DEVELOPMENTALISM

Gardner's theory is open to an objection that besets all forms of developmentalism. It is based on the central assumption that the unfolding with which we are familiar in the biological realm is also found in the mental. There are two problems about this, one for each of the two poles of alleged development, problems that we see illustrated in Gardner's own writings.

i) First the seed, or initial state. What is characteristic of biological seeds, including the union of sperm and egg at the beginning of human development, is that *they have within them the power to unfold* into more complex stages of their organic growth given the appropriate environmental conditions like air, light and water in the growth of a plant. To locate a parallel initial state in the mental case it is not enough simply to pick out innately given capacities. There is no doubt that such capacities exist. We are all born with the power to see and hear things, to move our bodies, to desire food and drink, to feel certain basic emotions like fear, to feel pain and pleasurable sensations. But we should not assume that any of the abilities just mentioned have within them the power to *unfold* into more complex forms of the same thing. I have italicized the word 'unfold' advisedly. For there is equally no doubt that the primitive capacities just mentioned do *change* into more sophisticated versions: the desire for food, for instance, becomes differentiated into desires for hamburgers and ice-cream; the brute ability to move one's limbs becomes specified into, for instance, the ability to run half-marathons or to tango. The changes wrought in these capacities are cultural products: people are socialized into them. This

social shaping cannot be characterized, as a defence of developmentalism might urge, as environmental conditions which have to be
satisfied for natural processes of growth to occur – the mental
equivalents of air, light and water in the growth of plants. For in the
latter case air, light and water are necessary for the innate propensities
to unfold from within, while the desires and capacities in question
become differentiated but do not unfold.

ii) The second problem concerns the other pole, the mature state to which
development tends. We can understand this notion well enough in
physical contexts like fully-grown hollyhocks or human bodies. A fully-
grown human body is one which can grow no further: it has reached
the limits of its development. The same is true of delphiniums and oak
trees. Like these, the human body can certainly go on *changing* , but
the changes are to do with the maintenance, and later deterioration, of
the system, not with its further growth. If we apply these ideas to the
mind, do we want to say that all human beings have mental ceilings –
e.g. in each of the areas of Gardner's intelligences – beyond which they
cannot progress? This goes against the grain for many teachers and
indeed for many laymen. They like to think of their intellectual life as
expandable and deepenable, in principle, in all sorts of directions. True,
psychologists of intelligence and the IQ have often built the notion of
mental ceilings into their notion of intelligence, but their views have
been trenchantly criticized over the last 30 years and more. (We will
come back to this in more detail.)

One answer to this might be that the development of intelligence is unlike
physical development in that here there are no ceilings, simply the potential
for endless growth in certain directions. Grounds would have to be provided,
of course, for this claim – which is tantamount to saying that mental
development fails to manifest a feature found in every other case of
development. But if we leave this on one side, the claim still includes the
idea of growth towards states of relative maturity, even if ceilings are not to

be found. It is not clear whether Gardner would embrace this claim. On the one hand he writes of 'end-state' performances (1983:64), which suggests finality; on the other, he describes the process of development in the intelligences as leading to 'exceedingly high levels of competence', which does not.

Whichever view he takes, he still has to answer the question: *what counts* as maturity in the case of the intelligences? In the case of the oak tree and the human body, we know when maturity has occurred through the use of our senses: over time we can see that a person is fully grown, physically speaking, or that an oak tree has reached its full dimensions. What equivalent is there in the mental realm? How do we know either that people have reached their mental ceiling or, on the ceiling-less view, that they are more mentally mature than they were?

We do not just use our senses. We cannot see a person's intellectual maturity as we can see that he or she is physically fully grown. So how *do* we tell?

In ordinary life we make all sorts of judgments about people's intellectual maturity or about how far they have got in their understanding of morality, say, or of the aesthetic. What is significant about these judgments is that they tend to be controversial. Some people would see intellectual maturity in *Mastermind* terms, as being able to marshal and remember heaps of facts; others would emphasize depth of understanding, yet others a synoptic grasp of connexions between many different fields, and so on. If we focus on a more specific area, like moral understanding, what counts as greater maturity here is similarly contentious. For some ex-ministers of education in the UK, this might be a matter of having seen the need to conform to certain absolute rules – that one should never lie, steal, break one's promises etc. Other people might put more weight on sensitivity to others' needs; others on a philosophical understanding of what morality is all about; others again on an awareness of the great plurality of moral values and the need to strike sensitive balances among them.

Ordinary judgments of mental or moral maturity like these do not exhibit the broad universality of agreement that we find in judgments about fully grown pine trees or badgers. This is because we are in the realm of value judgments rather than of observable facts. Judgers apply their intellectual and moral values to their decidings – and are likely to differ among themselves because of the different weights they each apply to the multiple criteria that operate in these areas.

Gardner's examples of high levels of development in the intelligences seem to reflect his own value judgments about what kinds of qualities are important. Remember, in this connexion, that a prerequisite for whether something counts as an intelligence is that it includes problem-solving skills which are useful and important within a cultural context. This is where Gardner starts from. He has in mind the achievements of outstanding poets, composers, religious leaders, politicians, scientists, novelists and so on. Would everyone agree with him that the poet is the best example of a person whose sensitivity to the meanings and other features of words has reached a high degree of perfection? Why not the philosopher? Or at least, if we remain within the aesthetic field, why not the connoisseur of poetry rather than its producer? Would everyone agree that the dancer, the actor, the athlete and the inventor best illustrate the higher levels of development in bodily-kinaesthetic intelligence? Why not the surgeon or the astronaut? Would everyone agree with the choice of Proust, Socrates, Jesus Christ, Mahatma Gandhi, Lyndon Johnson and Eleanor Roosevelt as prime examples in the sphere of the personal intelligences (taking the intrapersonal and the interpersonal together) (1983:239, 252)? Why not Nietzsche or Napoleon? (We shall return to this point below).

It seems, therefore, that the 'end states' of Gardner's intelligences are identified not by observation of what happens in nature, as in the development of plants or bodies, but by what is held – by Gardner – to be socially important. All of which provokes the thought: is 'development' not now a misnomer?

To conclude this section. I have tried to show that whether we look towards the beginning or towards the end of the development process, towards the seed or towards the full flowering, we find apparently insuperable problems in identifying mental counterparts to physical growth.

Since developmentalist assumptions are so central to Gardner's MI theory, the latter is seriously undermined.

'SUSCEPTIBILITY TO ENCODING IN A SYMBOL SYSTEM'

There is more to say about the prerequisite, just discussed, that to count as 'an intelligence' a candidate must be 'highly valued by cultures' (1983:61). A striking feature of Gardner's intelligences is that *aesthetic* considerations play so prominent a role in them. To recapitulate a little. Linguistic intelligence is manifested *par excellence* in the poet; musical, in the composer; spatial, in the painter and sculptor (as well as the scientist); bodily-kinaesthethic, in the dancer and actor (as well as the inventor and the athlete (who in our culture 'is trained in much the same way as an artistic performer' 1983:231)); intrapersonal, in the novelist (as well as the therapist, patient and wise elder). Only two of the seven intelligences are unconnected with forms of art: logico-mathematical, and interpersonal.

To some, not least educators who have taken it up in MI schools and elsewhere, it is an appealing feature of Gardner's theory that it associates intelligence so closely, although not exclusively by any means, with the arts. In broadening the notion beyond the linguistic and logico-mathematical types of thinking with which it has been traditionally associated, Gardner gives it a perceptible aesthetic bias. Why is this?

At this point we need to refer to one of Gardner's as yet unmentioned criteria of an intelligence, its 'susceptibility to encoding in a symbol system'. Gardner writes: 'following my mentor Nelson Goodman and other authorities, I conceive of a symbol as any entity (material or abstract) that can denote or refer to any other entity. On this definition, words, pictures, diagrams, numbers, and a host of other entities are readily considered symbols' (1983:301). In Gardner's view, symbols go beyond the world of the arts, being found also in logic, mathematics, the sciences and elsewhere. Yet artistic symbols plainly weigh heavily with him in his elaboration of MI theory. One reason for this is suggested in the Preface to *Frames of Mind* (1983:*viii*), where he describes the book as pulling together findings from earlier lines of research in the previous dozen years. 'One line is the development, in normal and gifted children, of symbol-using capacities, particularly in the arts.' Further light is thrown on this when one recalls that his mentor, Nelson Goodman, who examined differences between symbol systems, has been chiefly interested in symbol systems in the arts. (See his *Languages of Art* (Goodman, 1968); also Elgin, 1992.)

For Goodman a work of art is itself a symbol. Like a word, or a mathematical symbol, it refers to something in the world outside itself. It refers in different ways. A portrait refers to its sitter through representation. A sad piece of music refers to sadness in general by exemplifying this quality in itself. Aesthetic experience therefore gives us knowledge of what the world beyond the work is like: through attending to the details of the work we come to a more adequate understanding of what it symbolizes. Art is in this way a form of knowledge just like science or mathematics.

There are serious difficulties in Goodman's theory (see Scruton, 1974:221-6). Are works of art symbols in the way Goodman describes? If they refer to things outside themselves, just as words or mathematical symbols do, then we would expect the symbols involved to be translatable into other symbols. In English we use the word 'cat' to refer to a class of animals; Germans use their word 'Katze' to the same end. But it makes no sense to speak of translating a portrait of Henry VIII into some other equivalent symbol. Also, if the point of aesthetic experience is to attain knowledge of the world, how, as Ray Elliott has asked (Scruton 1974:226), can one explain why people go back again and again to a piece of music that they know very well? What they seek here is not necessarily more understanding of the world but reliving enjoyable experiences they have had in the past.

Goodman's cognitive account of the arts brings them too close to forms of knowledge proper like science or history. While a cognitive theory of art is rejected by aestheticians like Elliott, Scruton and Budd (referring to Suzanne Langer, Budd, 1985 ch.6), Gardner sees it as an advance on more inadequate conceptions. Writing (in Gardner, 1993b:135-7) about the influence of Goodman's cognitivism on him, he states:

In the wake of the pervasive cognitive revolution ..., it may be difficult to appreciate that this point of view was distinctly iconoclastic in its time. Evident among lay individuals, but also noticeable among art educators and theorists, was the belief that the arts were primarily a realm of emotion, mystery, magic or intuition. Cognition was associated with science or problem-solving, not with the creativity needed to fashion and appreciate artistic masterpieces. And even those who had some sympathy with a cognitive approach questioned whether an analysis in terms of 'those little things called symbols' could be productive. Nowadays, however, the battle has been largely won; those who would question the cognitive dimensions of the arts are themselves in a minority. (p.136)

On this last point, I think Gardner is plain wrong. The battle has not been won. While I can think of plenty of leading aestheticians who dismiss the approach of Goodman and like-minded thinkers, I am hard put to it to identify any major supporters.

If Goodman's account is problematic, then Gardner's MI theory, which depends on it, is similarly in jeopardy. But problems in Goodman aside, what is important for our present purposes is to realize that MI theory itself rests on another theory, Goodman's, and that the categorization of the different intelligences is tied to a categorization of different types of symbols – linguistic, mathematical, artistic etc – originating with this author. This helps to explain the apparently arbitrary, and otherwise seemingly inexplicable, collection of 'intelligences' that Gardner has brought together.

DO ALL THE INTELLIGENCES INVOLVE A SYMBOL SYSTEM?

This leads us to a further observation about MI theory. Do all the intelligences manifest the use of symbols, as the criterion of 'susceptibility to encoding in a symbol system' would suggest? If, for the sake of argument, we accepted Goodman's view that works of art are symbols which refer to the world, then linguistic intelligence – which is apotheosized in poetry – would certainly count. So would musical intelligence; and logico-mathematical; and spatial; and bodily-kinaesthetic; and intrapersonal – at least in so far as the hallmark of achievement in all these areas is the production of artistic or mathematical symbols. But what about interpersonal intelligence? What is produced here is nothing like a mathematical theory or a work of art, but a certain sort of social behaviour – to do, for instance, with 'influencing a group of disparate individuals to behave along desired lines' (p.239), in the way that religious and political leaders do. Of what is such behaviour a symbol? It is hard to make sense of this question. Yet the criterion in question would seem to expect some kind of answer to it.

Other areas than the interpersonal raise similar difficulties. Although, on Goodman's analysis, there are artistic symbols produced by bodily-kinaesthetic intelligence (dance, mime, drama), what shall we say of athletic achievements? Gardner strains hard to approximate them to artistic performances, but this is only one feature sometimes found in them, and then not usually the most important. In what way do the skilful performances in which tennis and snooker stars manifest their particular brand of intelligence symbolize by referring to something outside themselves?

All this may only seem a difficulty for Gardner on the assumption that each of the criteria furnishes necessary conditions for the existence of an intelligence. Gardner, as we shall see below, does not go as far as this: to count as an intelligence, only some, perhaps a majority, of the criteria have to apply. Perhaps, then, some forms of intelligence do not require the existence of symbols in the Gardner/Goodman sense.

If they do not, however, the question is left hanging why the term 'intelligence' should apply to them at all. Given that we can talk of the intelligent behaviour of footballers and politicians, what does such talk mean?

IDIOTS SAVANTS AND BRAIN LOCALIZATION

So far we have concentrated on two of Gardner's criteria

- a distinctive developmental history, along with a definable set of expert 'end-state' performances

- susceptibility to encoding in a symbol system.

Our discussion, especially of the former, has also brought in

- an identifiable core operation/set of operations.

Without going through all the remaining criteria, a word about two of them.

The existence in it of idiots savants and other exceptional individuals

I am not an expert on idiots savants, but what I know of them does not lead me to think of them as intelligent. Well known recent examples include an 11-year-old London boy who can draw complicated buildings perfectly having just seen them; a 23-year-old man who can play piano pieces perfectly having heard them only three times; and a young man who can tell you the day of the week of any date presented to him. All these cases are of subnormal mental ability. What they all have in common is a *mechanical* facility, one which lacks the flexibility of adaptation of means to ends found in intelligent behaviour.

The potential isolation of the area by brain damage

I am no expert either on the extent to which there are localized areas of function within the brain. But let us assume that there are to a marked degree. The question is: what would this show about the nature of intelligence? Suppose if one part of the brain is damaged, one cannot see, if another, one cannot move one's left hand, or feel pain, or talk, or understand language. What this would show is that certain physiological necessary conditions of exercizing these capacities were absent. It would not help to indicate the existence of separate 'intelligences'. No doubt some of these capacities enter into different kinds of intelligent performance: one could not play football intelligently without being able to move one's legs, or paint pictures without being able to see. But the capacities themselves are only elements in intelligent behaviour, not proto-intelligent capacities in themselves. Given his developmentalism, one can understand why Gardner should look to brain localization findings in order to identify intelligences, for he has to provide an account of the 'seed' which is to unfold into its mature form, and this seed has to be part of our original, biologically given, constitution. But the kinds of function picked out by brain localization research do not have the power, as far as I can see, to unfold into more developed forms. I am indeed born with the power of vision or the power to move my thumbs, but although various forms of socialization are built on these abilities, the latter do not themselves *grow* into maturer versions of themselves.

Finally, a comment about pain, i.e. physical pain like a toothache or the pain of a stab wound. We can all be anaesthetized not to feel it; and some people are born, I believe, without being able to experience it at all. Does this point towards some kind of separable pain intelligence on all fours with linguistic, spatial or bodily-kinaesthetic intelligence? What sense could we make of such a suggestion? Yet why is pain intelligence ruled out of the 'charmed circle' but these other items ruled in? Gardner could always respond, I suppose, that other criteria are not met: there is no developmental story in the case of toothaches, no headache geniuses, no Goodmanian symbols at work. But it seems to me that there is an obvious reason why the ability to feel pain is less close than, say, the ability to see, hear or move one's limbs to intelligent behaviour. The latter abilities are not separable forms of intelligence in themselves, but they are elements in larger patterns of intelligent ability. Intelligent tennis-playing, for instance, relies on all three of the examples just given. The ability to feel pain does not *facilitate* intelligent performances as these do: it can only get in the way of them, frustrate them.

In the last paragraph, as at earlier points in this critical discussion of MI theory, I have been assuming an alternative account of intelligence. Soon I shall have to bring this more into the open. But before that let me raise two further problems about Gardner's criteria.

HOW ARE THE CRITERIA TO BE APPLIED?

How does one use the criteria to pick out intelligences? If they were all necessary conditions, then each one of them would have to be met before we could say that an intelligence existed. This would give us a clear method of identification. Although some of them seem to be *necessary* – to judge by remarks like 'an intelligence must also be susceptible to encoding in a symbol system' (Gardner, 1990:933), in his original work Gardner makes it clear that not all have to be satisfied (Gardner, 1983:62). In places, the demand is more stringent. In his 1990 discussion of how he came to pick out his intelligences, he wrote that 'only those candidate intelligences that satisfied all or a majority of the criteria were selected as bona fide intelligences' (Gardner, 1990:932). If this is to be taken literally, then provided that five or more of the eight criteria listed are met, a candidate automatically passes the test. But it is clear from *Frames of Mind* that there is no 'algorithm for the selection of an intelligence, such that any trained researcher could determine whether a candidate intelligence met the appropriate criteria' (p.63). Rather, he goes on:

> it must be admitted that the selection (or rejection) of a candidate intelligence is reminiscent more of an artistic judgment than of a scientific assessment. (p.63)

I don't know if there is anything more to this admission than the thought that the identification of intelligences is a subjective matter, depending on the particular weightings that Howard Gardner gives to different criteria in different cases. If so, then his own value-preferences are likely to come into the story at some point. We have in fact seen some evidence of this in critical points earlier in this paper about the value he attaches to symbolic systems à la Goodman, especially in the aesthetic area.

WHY THESE CRITERIA?

A further – and surely fundamental – question is: how does Gardner justify using the particular criteria he lists to pick out intelligences?

I have not been able to find any answer in his writings.

A GLOBAL VERDICT

The overall verdict on MI theory must be that it is seriously deficient as an account of intelligence. It seems to rest at root on the insecurest of foundations, dependent on subjective judgments on Gardner's part. It takes the shape it does partly because it is based on two further theories, Piagetian-style developmentalism and a Goodman-style theory of symbolism, both of which themselves rest on shaky foundations.

In several ways MI theory diverges from our everyday understanding of intelligent behaviour. As was earlier stated, this has to do with adopting efficient means to attain one's goals, flexibly varying these according to circumstances. Different kinds of activities have different goals and ways of attaining them: intelligence displayed in archaeological digs is different from that found in flying a jet plane, planning a day's outing, making a soufflé. Archaeological digs are themselves various, of course, dependent on different purposes and requiring different *modi operandi*. The same is true for flying jet planes. It is unlikely that the enormous variety found in human means-end behaviour can be regimented into a small number of logical categories.

But at least this way of looking at intelligence puts the primary focus on the part it plays in practical reasoning of different sorts – rather than, say, on intelligence focused more narrowly on the subset of academic pursuits. Intelligence is not all there is to practical reasoning, of course, as we saw earlier in Aristotle's distinction between the practically wise person and the merely clever one (*Nicomachean Ethics*, Bk.6). Intelligence or cleverness has to do only with the adequacy of means to ends: it does not touch the adequacy of the ends themselves. A hit-man can be as astute as you like in the pursuit of evil ends.

There is more to be said about our ordinary understanding of intelligence – about how far the term is rightly applied to other animals, for instance, or how far it squares with the concept of intelligence used by IQ theorists (White and Ryle, 1974; Winch, 1990, chs.4-6). We will come back to some of these issues in 'Intelligence and the IQ', below.

In his introduction to the second (1993a) edition of *Frames of Mind*, Gardner makes two revealing comments. First, that

> intelligences by themselves are neither pro-social nor antisocial. Goethe used his linguistic intelligence for positive ends, Goebbels his for destructive ones; Stalin and Gandhi both understood other individuals, but put their interpersonal intelligences to diverse uses. (1993a:*xxviii*)

This is essentially Aristotle's point about cleverness and challenges the account in the first edition, where the highest levels of development in intelligence were all couched in positive terms, to do with achievements highly valued within a culture. (See the remark on this, p.11 above.)

The second comment is this.

> In *Frames of Mind*, I stressed the extent to which intrapersonal intelligence grew out of, and was organized around, the 'feeling life' of the individual. If I were to rework the relevant parts of chapter 10 today, I would stress instead the importance of having a viable model of oneself and of being able to draw effectively upon the model in making decisions about one's life. (p.*xxii*)

This is a welcome nudge towards acknowledging the role of intelligence in the practical organization of our lives as individuals.

In both these revisions Gardner comes a little closer to the everyday concept of intelligence. Among other things the shift of position shows the importance of prior philosophical reflection on conceptual connexions for any psychologist working on a theoretical account of some aspect of mental life. If Gardner had had his 1993a insights ten years earlier, the original MI theory could not have taken quite the shape it did. If, in addition, he had subjected his developmentalist and symbol-theory assumptions to philosophical critique, the original theory probably could not have even reached the drawing board.

Intelligence and the IQ: an alternative to Gardner's theory

A main theme of this paper has been that while Gardner is right to challenge the identification of intelligence with what IQ tests test and to claim that it takes more varied forms than the linguistic and logico-mathematical abilities required by those tests, he goes adrift when he tries to pigeonhole this variety within his seven or eight boxes. In this section I shall try to fill out the everyday idea of multiple intelligences introduced earlier as an alternative to Gardner's concept. Among other things, this will, I hope, throw more light on the inadequacy of the IQ test.

VARIETIES OF INTELLIGENCE

It has already been claimed (p.4, above) that intelligent action has to do with the flexible adaptation of means in the pursuit of one's goals. Since there are an indefinite number of human goals, intelligence can be displayed in countless different ways. Instances were given of bowlers varying their delivery to dispatch a batsman, of car drivers adjusting to the situation on the road ahead of them, of thinking through possibilities when planning a holiday.

Intelligence is popularly connected with skill in reasoning; but it is only in the last of these three examples that reasoning occupies a central place. When you plan a holiday, you have to think things through. 'Switzerland would be idyllic for walking ... but it's expensive ... and July could be wet ... who was it talking about North Portugal?' No doubt some trains of thought on this pattern can go on when driving on the motorway ('Why are they all slowing down? Roadworks ahead? Or accident? In any case, I'd better follow suit'). More typically, however, the varying actions which the driver takes in proceeding towards her destination are more immediate than that: she sees a red tail light ahead, a car coming into her lane, a derestriction sign and automatically, as it were, slows down, pulls out, accelerates. Not that what she does is automatic in the sense that a washing machine works automatically once switched on. She has a mind and a washing machine does not. It is important to note that she has to see something happening in order to produce the reaction she does: her consciousness is at work. In this case her consciousness does not take the form of thinking something through, but of seeing something and acting accordingly. Her long experience of driving has provided her with a number of repertoires, of habitual responses to situations which obviate the need for reasoning. If asked after the event, 'Why did you slow down just now?' she will be able to reply 'Because I saw the cars ahead slow down'. If she were unable to give some such answer we might indeed begin to doubt that she had acted intelligently. But no reasoning-through was necessary at the time: reliance on her learnt repertoires was sufficient.

I have dwelt on this example partly with a view to undermining the IQ view of intelligence. IQ tests test how good a person is at a certain sort of reasoning. They do not test the intelligence shown by drivers, or bowlers, or tennis players, or marksmen, in which reasoning occupies a small place. But then neither do they test all forms of reasoning – they exclude that employed by our holiday planner, for instance. It is only certain kinds of reasoning to which they attend, those typically of a mathematical or logical sort.

Why is logico-mathematical thought privileged by the IQ test? A full answer to this question would have to take us into the contingencies of the history of IQ testing, but the reason is surely not unconnected with the deeply embedded belief within our (western) culture that the highest type of thinking is also the most abstract. Descartes held this view; and 2,000 years before him, so did Plato. In each of their cases it was connected with the belief that the essential element in human personhood is the mind or soul, not the body: when the body dies, the soul lives on. There is no need here to go into the further connexions between this view and – in Descartes's case – a specifically Christian picture of human life to see why tennis playing or car driving can be sidelined in the intelligence stakes, or why it comes so naturally to some of us to place these, in the hierarchy of intelligent behaviour we may carry around in our heads, lower than holiday planning and the latter lower than mathematical or philosophical thinking. For driving and tennis playing rely heavily on physical skills and thus on our existence as embodied beings. Planning a holiday is something we can do with much less physical activity. Reasoning becomes prominent here, as we have seen. Yet it is still reasoning enmeshed in the embodied world – the world of mountain walking, sightseeing, sun, Sangria and what you will. It is only when we pass to the abstractions, the conceptual interrelationships of pure – as distinct from applied – mathematics or formal logic that we reach forms of thought whose subject matter is minimally attached to our everyday, bodily existence.

HUMDRUM INTELLIGENCE

It may be felt that an account of intelligence in terms of flexible behaviour in relation to one's goals is too weak to do justice to the way we use the term. Suppose I come home from work and try to unlock my front door. At first I find myself using the garage key, so I switch to the house key. Then I can't get this key into the keyhole because it is upside down, so I turn it round the right way. In all this I am behaving flexibly, varying what I do to the situation; but who on earth, seeing all this, would say 'Gracious, how intelligent!' ? This is because we usually only call behaviour 'intelligent' if it in some way transcends normal expectations, if, for instance, a person applies her understanding in judgments which are abnormally quick or abnormally sophisticated. This objection focuses on the kinds of occasions when we use the word 'intelligent'. But it is not clear how much light observations of this sort throw on the meaning of a concept. To take another example. We talk about people's motives when there is, or may be, something untoward about what they are doing: we ask for the motives of a criminal, but not of a man going into a restaurant. But the fact that we would never *talk* about people's motives for the quite ordinary and readily intelligible things they do does not imply that they do not *have* motives for these things. The man's motive in going into the restaurant is his desire to satisfy his hunger. The very obviousness of the motive explains why we have no need to mention it. We must beware of the same fallacy (which Searle (1970:141 ff) calls 'the assertion fallacy') in writing into the meaning of 'intelligence' something to do with transcending normal expectations. Putting a key in a door is never *called* 'intelligent', but this does not imply that it *is not* intelligent. Once again, it is the very obviousness of its being an intelligent thing to do which makes it not worth saying that it is. Intelligent performances, like actions from motives, are such omnipresent features of our lives that it is scarcely surprising that we do not often trouble to call them what they are.

NON-INTELLIGENCE, LACKING AN ABILITY, AND UNINTELLIGENCE

As we saw earlier, Gardner's idea that intelligence is not necessarily tied to IQ-tested skills has had a liberating effect on children, often from deprived backgrounds, who think of themselves as 'thick' or 'dim'. One thing often presupposed to such thinking is that thickness or dimness belongs to the sort of person one is, that it is runs through one like the word 'Blackpool' through a stick of rock. But is this how we should see things?

Some things are not intelligent at all – paperclips, boulders, loaves of bread. We could have added daisies and sequoias to this list and perhaps spiders and clams as well, but instead of climbing further up the phylogenetic tree to animals like rabbits and antelopes where some kind of intelligence in the form of flexible behaviour seems undeniable, let us stay well clear of the gradations of the biological world and concentrate on our plainly intelligence-less paperclips and rocks.

Now when we say a paperclip lacks intelligence, we are surely not saying that it is thick or stupid or unintelligent. We are dealing with a different sort of contrast. To see matters clearly, we need in fact to make a three-fold distinction.

i) Paperclips and rocks are not unintelligent; they are non-intelligent. That is to say, they do not have the wherewithal ever to be able to display flexible goal-directed behaviour. They are constitutionally incapable of it, being not made of the right kind of material. Human beings and doubtless some other animals are – nearly always – born with the ability to acquire flexible forms of behaviour as they grow up.

They are intelligent creatures in a way that filing cabinets and sausages are not. To say they are intelligent is to say that they are constitutionally – genetically – equipped with the ability, or capacity, to acquire such skills as speaking, playing hockey, driving cars, planning holidays, doing algebra and an unlimited host of others things.

ii) Someone who has learned to drive has acquired a form of intelligence which a non-driver does not possess – they can appropriately adapt their behaviour to road conditions as earlier described. Both driver and non-driver are intelligent creatures as outlined in *i)*, in that they are both born with the capacity to acquire a skill like driving. Only the driver manifests driving intelligence. How then shall we characterize the non-driver? In a way he is lacking in intelligence. In what way? Not, as we have seen, in the paperclip's way: he is not a non-intelligent creature. Is the non-driver's lack of intelligence equatable with unintelligence? Surely not. We are not saying that just because he has not learnt how to drive he is stupid or a dimwit. His lack of intelligence is simply his not possessing the skill in question. We all lack intelligence in this sense in a million and one ways. Children from deprived backgrounds often lack intelligence in many areas where their more fortunate coevals are already adept. This is not at all to say they are 'thick'.

iii) The final contrast is between intelligence and unintelligence or stupidity. It is embarrassing and demeaning to have to admit it, but a year or so ago when I was trying to fix a leaking tap, I managed to project an unstoppable jet of scalding water across the kitchen and tried vainly to get near enough to smother it in a wodge of teatowels and handtowels. If I'd thought for a moment and not panicked, I would have remembered to turn on the upstairs taps to reduce the pressure. It was really stupid not to do so.

We are all stupid from time to time. Stupidity consists in a lapse, a failure. One *has* the relevant skills – knowing how to control the water system in my own case – but fails to apply them on a particular occasion. Just as lacking intelligence in sense *ii)* presupposes possessing intelligence in sense *i)*, so lacking intelligence in sense *iii)* presupposes being intelligent in sense *ii)*.

All this bolsters the claim that stupidity does not run through one like letters through rock. Children may sometimes think of themselves as thickos, but they are logically awry in doing so. Stupidity is not a personal quality, on a par with such vices as meanness or inolerance. It is not an enduring feature of one's personality, but a one-off or occasional failure – through tiredness, anxiety, panic or whatever – to activate the know-how one possesses.

We have, then, three concepts of intelligence, a distinction we owe originally, and in a somewhat different form, to Aristotle's *De Anima* (II. 5., 417A 21). Beginning with the clearly biological one, we have *i)* intelligence as the innate capacity to acquire specific intelligent abilities or capacities. Its opposite is non-intelligence.

ii) intelligence in an area as a specific capacity (to forage for food, to swim, to drive etc.). Its opposite is the non-possession of the capacity in question.

iii) intelligence as the realization, the successful application, of a specific capacity in a particular instance. Its opposite, stupidity or unintelligence, is a failure to apply this capacity.

THE NATURE-NURTURE DEBATE AND THE MILK-BOTTLE ACCOUNT OF INTELLIGENCE

How far do these distinctions help us in sorting out the 'nature-nurture' problem? It looks as if there may be a pretty simple solution to it. Is intelligence an innate capacity? Well, doesn't it depend on which concept one takes? Intelligence as the capacity to acquire capacities – the first sense – is clearly innate; intelligence in the other two senses is acquired. (Debates over general intelligence can be defused, it seems, in the same way. Is intelligence general or specific? The intelligence that human beings have and rocks do not is a general ability to acquire abilities; acquired abilities and their successful realization are multiple and specific.)

It would be gratifying to think one could dispatch the 'nature-nurture' issue as quickly as this. But it would be odd if one could. For it would be surprising in the extreme if this long-standing controversy which has generated so much heat and so many millions of learned words, turned on no more than a simple ambiguity in the word 'intelligence'.

The controversy, in fact, goes deeper than this. To see this, take the claim, deriving originally from Francis Galton in the nineteenth century, found notably in Cyril Burt's writings in the early twentieth, and is now the basis of *The Bell Curve* arguments today (Herrnstein and Murray, 1994), that intelligence is an innate capacity of some sort – in Burt's formulation, that it is 'innate, general, cognitive ability'. Now, despite appearances, it is clear,

27

I think, that intelligence as so defined is not intelligence in the first of the three Aristotelian senses, i.e. is not intelligence as the (innate) capacity to acquire capacities. For intrinsic to the Galtonian concept of intelligence is that individuals may differ in this intelligence: one person may be more intelligent than another. The notion of possible degrees of intelligence is not written into the concept of intelligence as the (innate) capacity to acquire capacities. Animals, including human beings, either have this capacity or they do not. Human beings (in almost all cases) have it.

There is an important linguistic point to make here, so as to avoid a possible confusion. I have claimed, against Galton or Burt, that normally human beings do not differ in innate capacity. But 'capacity' is an ambiguous word. In one sense, it simply means 'power': men are born with the power of acquiring learned abilities, a power not found in plants and rocks. But in another sense, it means more than this. In saying, for instance, that a milk bottle has a 'capacity' of one pint, I am implying not merely that it has the power of holding one pint, but also, more importantly, that it *lacks the power to hold more than this*. There are upper limits, if you like, on the amount it can hold.

The Galtonian concept of intelligence sees it as an innate capacity in the latter of these two senses. We are born not simply with conceptual powers, but with individually varying mental ceilings beyond which we cannot develop.

We can each hold only just so much intellectual substance; some of us may be quart-size, as it were, others pint-size, others quarter-pint-size. An example of such a conception of intelligence is found in a paper of Cyril Burt's, written in 1955 and abridged in Wiseman (1967). Having defined intelligence as 'an innate, general, cognitive factor', Burt goes on to add:

> The degree of intelligence with which any particular child is endowed is one of the most important factors determining his general efficiency all throughout life. In particular it sets an upper limit to what he can successfully perform, especially in the educational, vocational and intellectual fields. (Wiseman, 1967:280-1)

We are back with the view which we looked at briefly when examining the developmentalist assumptions in MI theory in an earlier section, that human beings have mental ceilings beyond which they cannot progress.

I cannot stress too strongly the difference between this Galtonian/Burtian concept of intelligence and the first of my 'Aristotelian' senses. To say, in the Aristotelian way, that we have an innate capacity to acquire learned abilities does not imply that there is any upper limit, peculiar to the individual, on the abilities attainable. It does not imply an innate capacity in the milk-bottle sense of 'capacity'. It may be true that in one sense we must be limited in what we can achieve. If one agrees with Kant's (1781) thesis in his *Critique of Pure Reason*, we must all be limited, as far as our theoretical knowledge goes, to what falls within the bounds of our possible experience. If so, being an intelligent creature, i.e. having the innate capacity to acquire specific abilities, *does* imply upper limits of a sort. This is a conceptual truth, establishable *a priori*. But the Kantian claim is different from the Galtonian one, in that there is no mention in Kant of the possibility of *individual differences* in one's upper limits. The limits are the same for all of us. In the Galtonian conception, however, we each have our own, individually distinctive, innately produced ceiling of potential.

Now that we have separated out the Galtonian conception from others with which it is too easily confused, we can examine it more closely. This, as we shall see, will take us into the heart of the 'nature-nurture' issue. Intelligence, on this Galtonian view, is innate cognitive capacity in the 'milk-bottle' sense.

THE THEOLOGY OF THE IQ

The crucial problem now is: does intelligence in this Galtonian sense exist? Clearly we cannot take it that it does without evidence. What kind of evidence would be necessary to confirm or refute this claim? At this point we need to break down the claim into two component parts: *i)* that for each of us there are upper limits of intellectual development (which may differ from individual to individual) and *ii)* that these upper limits are fixed by an *innate* capacity (called 'intelligence'). Both of these sub-claims require evidence.

Let me concentrate – in this paper – on the first. What criteria would have to be satisfied to show that a person has an upper limit in this sense (regardless, for the moment, of how this limit is produced)? Poor achievement on its own would clearly not be a criterion. If a child fails to understand a certain theorem in geometry – Pythagoras's perhaps – we cannot assume such understanding to be forever beyond him. He may well come to grasp it tomorrow perhaps because his teacher has tried to explain it to him in a different way, or for some other reason. But suppose all sorts of teaching methods are tried and none of them work. Would *this* be sufficient to show that he had reached a ceiling? Is there not still always the possibility that some method may work of which we are not now aware? I suppose there always is. But it seems to me that, beyond a certain point (and I am not clear where that point is) doubts like this may become otiose. Some children with severe learning difficulties do seem to have intellectual ceilings, in that they are unable to acquire even a rudimentary grasp of language. Here the evidence is the failure of all sorts of different methods of helping them over this hurdle. Perhaps this evidence is insufficient. If so, one might conclude that the claim that at least some people have upper intellectual limits is *unverifiable* . I do not think I want to say this.

But the Galtonian claim is in any case stronger than this: not that some, but that all of us are so limited. Is *this* a verifiable proposition? One difficulty is that this now applies to normal individuals as well as those with severe learning difficulties: and with normals it is so much more difficult to tell when the criterion I have been urging has been satisfied because they possess a conceptual equipment which teachers can make use of in trying to devise different methods of getting them over intellectual hurdles. It is not clear to me just when, if at all, one would be justified in concluding that a normal individual had reached his ceiling and that no further teaching efforts would be of any use.

A second difficulty over the verifiability of the claim that *all* have ceilings is that it seems that there must be at least one person whose ceilings cannot be shown (always assuming that ceilings in general can be determined). For to establish that a person has a ceiling one must have failed in attempts to get him or her beyond this ceiling – which implies that one can oneself operate conceptually beyond this point. So there must always be at least one person of whom it cannot be shown that he has a ceiling. For if there were no such person, then who could have shown that the person or persons with the highest ceiling had such a ceiling?

It looks, therefore, as if the claim we are examining is in principle unverifiable. But neither does it seem to be in principle *falsifiable*. For what could possibly falsify the proposition that we all have intellectual ceilings? Nothing, as far as I can see. It one took the most brilliant person in the world, whose grasp of new ideas seemed boundless, even this would not be enough to falsify it. Even she, clearly, might have her *Pons Asinorum* somewhere, even though no one could ever know what it was.

If this argument is correct, the proposition that we all have our own upper limits of ability is both unverifiable and unfalsifiable in principle. So, too, therefore, is the proposition that we all have innately determined upper limits, i.e. that there is such a thing as Galtonian intelligence. So too, indeed, is the more specific claim that we all have upper limits which vary along a normal curve. To say that these propositions are unverifiable and unfalsifiable in principle is to underline that they cannot be *empirical* hypotheses and therefore subject-matter for scientific investigation. They are, rather, metaphysical speculations in the Kantian sense that they transcend the bounds of any possible experience. Positivists might claim that they are meaningless utterances. Not holding a verifiability theory of meaning, I would not want to go as far as this. But in their unverifiability and unfalsifiability, they are similar to the claim that there is always some unconscious motive for what we do, a hypothesis which some Freudians might hold. Or to the claim that every historical event has been preordained by God, or is the product of economic forces. Or to the claim that Jesus Christ was the Son of God. All of these claims, as far as I can see, *might* be true. But no possible evidence could prove them right or prove them wrong.

Propositions of this kind are often found at the centre of ideological systems of belief, e.g. Marxism, Christianity, psychoanalytic theory. This is not surprising. To say that a proposition like 'God exists' cannot be falsified is to say that no one can produce any good reason for claiming that it is not true, or if you like, it is to say that its truth cannot rationally be denied. But if its truth cannot rationally be denied, its truth is surely undeniable. In which case one might be inclined to conclude it surely must be true.

This line of thought may help to explain why adherents of different ideological systems often cling so tenaciously to their beliefs, even where these depend on unverifiable propositions like the one mentioned. But it is, of course, fallacious. What is undeniable in the sense that it cannot be falsified is not necessarily undeniable in the sense that it *must be true* .

Like the religious and political propositions I have mentioned, the proposition that we all have innately determined upper intellectual limits has become the hub of a new ideological system. Around it, too, have accreted all kinds of other propositions, both descriptive, for instance about the constancy of IQ, normal distributions and so on, and prescriptive, for example about the different kinds of educational provision which ought to be made for children of different 'innate capacities'. As such a system grows in complexity, and the more its supporters occupy themselves with discussions about the details of the more peripheral parts of the system, the greater the likelihood that the basic beliefs, presupposed to these peripheral ones, get taken for granted and so made all the harder to question or relinquish. If two people, for instance, are arguing whether God is one person or three, they are each committed to the belief that God exists. If two others are arguing whether one's IQ is a valid indication of one's intellectual ceiling, they are each committed to the belief that we have such ceilings.

Gardner's multiple intelligences and Hirst's forms of knowledge

To come back, finally, to Gardner's theory of multiple intelligences and its impact on educational reform. In some ways both it and its educational fate are reminiscent of Paul Hirst's earlier (1965) theory of the 'forms of knowledge' and its take-up by the educational establishment. Hirst's is a theory of the content of a liberal education, understood as an education pursued for intrinsic ends and not for extrinsic, e.g. vocational, reasons. This content is divided into seven areas of understanding, identified by the application of certain epistemological criteria: each area must have its own peculiar concepts and tests for truth. The forms of understanding definitely identified are (in the original version): mathematics, the natural sciences, the human sciences, history, philosophy, moral knowledge, literature and the fine arts. What students acquire in each area is not a collection of facts, but a way of thinking. Hirst's theory was taken up by educational policy makers from school to national level, many of whom held that school curricula should ensure engagement with the seven types of thinking.

Gardner's original theory is also based on seven forms of thought, identified by explicit criteria – not epistemological in this case but an amalgam of criteria based largely on brain physiology, developmental psychology and a theory of symbols. It, too, has been applied to education, first by Gardner himself and then by educational reformers of many kinds. In a recent *Times Educational Supplement* interview (17.3.95), Gardner was asked whether he thought 'every child should be given chances to develop every mode of intelligence'. Without committing himself definitely to this view, he stated 'Many of the people who are on the MI bandwagon believe that, and who's to say they are wrong?'

Curiously, both Hirst's and Gardner's theory have the same grey area, where each writer is not clear-cut about whether to admit a particular candidate into the favoured circle. Hirst was unsure from the start whether there is a distinctive form of religious understanding. In his restatement, Gardner writes:

> Those interested in the evolution of the theory of multiple intelligence since 1983 often ask whether additional intelligences have been added – or original candidates deleted. The answer is that I have elected not to tamper for now with the original list, though I continue to think that some form of 'spiritual intelligence' may well exist. (1993a:*xxii*)

(As stated previously, Gardner has also recently come to think that there may be a separate naturalist's intelligence, to do with classifying forms of animal and plant life.)

It is understandable that teachers and policy-makers should have reacted to these two theories in the way they have. If a leading academic authority identifies a small number of crucial forms of thinking/ understanding/ intelligence – either, as in Gardner's case, as fundamental to human nature as such, or in Hirst's, as fundamental to a rational existence in modern cultural conditions – many educators are likely to try to ensure that their charges are not deprived of something so basic to their flourishing.

Another reason why the two theories have struck a chord with the educational world may be that both sets of favoured categories are of forms of thought closer to the intellectual life than to more practical and everyday forms of human existence. Among other things, both theories have worked with a cognitive conception of the arts, which has assimilated them to those curriculum subjects concerned with the pursuit of truth. Hirst's forms are akin, with the exception of moral knowledge, to disciplines found in a traditional university or sixth form. Gardner's intelligences cover much of the same ground, with a special weighting, as we have seen towards the arts – except that they extend more widely than Hirst's forms, interpersonal intelligence, for instance, dealing with the intellectual qualities of political and religious leadership.

As Ryle (1949) memorably reminded us in *The Concept of Mind* , and as we have seen above, intelligent behaviour is not confined to intellectual matters but extends into all areas of practical reasoning and beyond. Hirst's more recent thinking about the content of education has jettisoned the approach via intellectual disciplines and is now founded on initiation into a range of 'social practices', in which practical reasoning takes pride of place (see, for example, Hirst, 1993). Gardner's (1993a) revisions show some slight shift in the same direction. Whatever the changes in his thinking in the future, he would do well to follow Hirst's – or for that matter Wittgenstein's – example and begin from a wholly different starting point.

Conclusion

Gardner's success in opening teachers' and project workers' eyes to new possibilities deserves our gratitude. It is aided by the fresh and accessible way in which he presents his ideas. But there are dangers in taking MI theory on board. The seven or eight categories are too close to familiar curricular areas for comfort. They make curriculum planning deceptively easy. They tempt us to bypass the complex ethical and practical problems found in constructing a defensible curriculum in favour of a categorization backed by all the authority of a Harvard professor. We may escape the shackles of IQ intelligence only to find ourselves imprisoned within another dubious theory.

'How many of your intelligences have you used today?' Let's not inflict this question on children from deprived inner city schools where MI theory is currently making most impact. It would be stupid to do so.

Note

I am very grateful to Anna Craft for discussions on Howard Gardner's theory, especially on his most recent views. I would also like to thank her and Brahm Norwich for their helpful comments on a draft of this paper. I am most indebted to Richard Worth, Maggie Farrar and Professor John MacBeath for their accounts of school improvement projects in which Howard Gardner's work has proved a catalyst, in Sandwell, Birmingham and Glasgow respectively.

Part of the section on 'Intelligence and the IQ' originally appeared in White (1974). I am grateful to Gilbert Ryle's reply to my paper in the same symposium for making me see problems in the account of the concept of intelligence I presented there. These ideas have been reworked for the present essay.

REFERENCES

Aristotle *De Anima*

— *Nicomachean Ethics*

Budd, M. (1985), *Music and the Emotions: the philosophical theories* London: Routledge & Kegan Paul.

Craft, A. (1997), *Proceedings of Creativity in Education Colloquium on Multiple Intelligences and creativity with Professor Howard Gardner, July 1997*. Milton Keynes: Open University School of Education

Elgin, C.Z. (1992), 'Goodman, Nelson' in D. Cooper (ed.) *A Companion to Aesthetics*. Oxford: Blackwell.

Gardner, H. (1983), *Frames of Mind* London: Heinemann.

— (1990), 'The theory of multiple intelligences' in N. Entwistle (ed.) *Handbook of Educational Ideas and Practices*. London: Routledge.

— (1993a), *Frames of Mind* (Second Edition), London: Fontana.

— (1993b), *Multiple Intelligences: the theory in practice*. New York: Basic Books.

Goodman, N. (1968), *Languages of Art*. Indianapolis: Hackett.

Hamlyn, D.W. (1978), *Experience and the growth of understanding*. London: Routledge & Kegan Paul.

Herrnstein, R. and Murray, A. (1994), *The Bell Curve : intelligence and class structure in American life*. London: Free Press.

Hirst, P (1965), 'Liberal Education and the Nature of Knowledge' in R.D. Archambault (ed.) *Philosophical Analysis and Education*. London: Routledge & Kegan Paul.

— (1993), 'Education, knowledge and practices' in R. Barrow and P. White (eds), *Beyond Liberal Education: Essays in Honour of Paul H. Hirst*. London: Routledge.

Kant, I. (1781), *The Critique of Pure Reason*.

Ryle, G. (1949), *The Concept of Mind*. London: Hutchinson.

Searle, J.R. (1970), *Speech Acts*. Cambridge: Cambridge University Press.

Scruton, R. (1974), *Art and Imagination*. London: Methuen.

White, J. and Ryle, G. (1974), Symposium on 'Intelligence and the Logic of the Nature-Nurture Issue' in *Proceedings of the Philosophy of Education Society of Great Britain* Vol VIII No1.

Winch, C. (1990), *Language, Ability and Educational Achievement*. New York: Routledge.

Wiseman, S. (1967), (ed.) *Intelligence and Ability*. Harmondsworth: Penguin Books.